Biographies of the Masters

1

First published in Italian as, *Śaṅkara*, by Edizioni Āśram Vidyā, Rome, Italy.

ISBN 978-1-931406-11-6

Front Cover: Ādi Śaṅkara

ŚAṄKARA

AUREA VIDYĀ

Knowledge adorns those cultivating it, but in the case of Śaṅkara it was Knowledge which was adorned by him.

Mādhavīyaśaṅkaravijaya

One must discern between Being and being this or that, between the "I am that which I am" and the "I am this or that", between the unveiling without name and form and living for the name and the form. Only an act of profound discernment can make us recognize the essential nature of our own true Being.

Raphael

ŚAṄKARA

This publication is a homage to Śaṅkara, the great *advaitin*, one of the most representative philosophical minds of India, who has realized the most complete synthesis and harmonization of the entire Indian philosophical thought. His "method" for researching Truth, which essentially consists in liberating it from the veils that cover it, has given a truly valuable contribution to the philosophical-metaphysical thought of the entire world.

Śaṅkara has realized a perfect synthesis of knowledge (*jñāna*), devotion (*bhakti*), and action (*karma*); this allows him to offer, to those approaching Realization, the way that best responds to their qualifications.

He incarnated in such a perfect way the "Supreme Knowledge" (*paravidyā*) that a verse of the *Mādhaviyaśaṅkaravijaya* recites: «Knowledge adorns those cultivating it, but in the case of Śaṅkara it was Knowledge which was adorned by him».

For all the great beings who have incarnated a Principle of universal order so as to offer Humanity a way of Knowledge, of Love and of Realization – like the Buddha, Jesus and Śaṅkara – their birth, life, works and also their "passing away" have always been clothed in a halo of myth and of legend. There exists their "historical" figure and the written works which have come down to us from them directly or through their disciples, but we do not have the exact dates of their birth and of their "death".

One can also note how there are points of convergence, at times of similarity, between the various biographies of these Great Souls, even if their descent has taken place in times and in contexts very different from each other.

We think that all this is there to indicate that for these transmitters of the one Source the individual aspects of their lives need not be researched. It is not to the physical form or to their individuality we have to look, but to the Doctrine which they expressed through that physical form, to the Teaching they brought to a Humanity in conflict in order to "overcome the world", the world of shadows, the world of becoming and to reconquer the "Dignity of Being".

It is not, therefore, with an analytical mind, always looking for notions and personal "data", that the works of a Buddha, of a Śaṅkara or the Gospel of Jesus can be read, but with a mind open to receiving a beneficial influence, even if in the form of myth or legend. Truly these are the ways of "telling" the reality which allow the mind to overcome its own "human" limitations, and to draw us near to the Divine: «..."certain things" are overhistorical, they belong to a sole Source... Some "myths" about people and facts are not dead, but simply asleep. It would be a slight thing to bring them back again into the open, if one just possessed the kind of inspiration that derives from that Source».

Before being born

Śaṅkara's biographies normally open with a solemn prologue beyond this world, on the sublime peak of Mount Kailāsa, Śiva's sacred abode in the depth of all beings... The scene is therefore Kailāsa; there Śiva is seated in the radiance of his undivided consciousness, in love-union with his transcendent power (*Paraśakti*), Mother of the world and creating Word. Around him, the host of the praising devotees: the immortal seers (*Ṛṣi*), the perfect ones (*Siddha*), those who have identified with Him in order to become in their turn "Himself" (*Rudra*), and the faithful servants tormenting his enemies.

Moved by the prayers of the seer Nārada, messenger between the world of humans and that of the Gods, Brahmā, the demiurge who at Śiva's command has forged the universe, goes in His presence. Prostrating himself, he remains mute, rapt in contemplation.

Invited to speak, *Brahmā* depicts the conditions of the world, portraying it in bleak colors: *Kaliyuga*, the age of decadence and of pain, is by now acting in its full corrupting power: erroneous doctrines have spread everywhere clouding the consciousness of the majority from the immemorial truth of the *Veda* and *Vedānta*. Men are dragged into wicked actions, outside of the path of righteousness (*Dharma*), humble moths attracted by the terrible flame of the false pleasures of appearances. The time has come to keep with the ancient promise. The descent of the Lord in the Bhāratavaṣa, the land of India, in order to establish there anew the *Advaita*'s pure truth founding there again the *Dharma* and allowing humanity a new moment of light! Śiva had solemnly made this commitment thousands of years before, in the presence of his Power and of his divine hosts. Śiva gave his consent with a smile. But the descent (*avatāra*) of the Master of all beings must be prepared by other descents. In order to re-establish the sanctity of the *Veda*, the fight against false ideas will be initiated by the head of the celestial armies, Kumāra son of Śiva himself, who will be born as a man in the person of Kumārila, and become the champion of the *Pūrvamīmāṁsā* school of thought. Indra, king of the gods (*deva*) always ready to fight for the right cause against the forces of ill, will give him the support of the temporal power, being born in the person of *rāja* Sudhanvabhūti. To co-operate with Śiva divine disciples will be necessary to continue the teaching among men: Brahmā himself will be born as Maṇḍana, and his divine spouse Sarasvatī, mistress of knowledge, as a mortal woman in order that she can continue to be next to him, keeping the same name: *Viṣṇu*, principle of the cohesion and conservation of the universal order, will descend among men in the person of Sananda. The Lord of the waters Varuṇa, will be born as Citsukha; the Lord of fire, Agni, as Ānandagiri; that of the air, Vāyu, as Hastāmalaka. Also Mṛtyu, personified Death, and Yama the Lord of the deceased will also contribute, the former taking birth as Pṛthivīdhara, the latter as Viśvarūpa, both destined to become disciples of Śiva. The parts have been given, the divine actors are wearing their masks: everything is ready for the protagonist to come forward and for the event to begin.

His Life

According to the hagiographers, at the end of the seventh century a head of family (*gṛhastha*) named Nambūṭiri was living in Kālaṭi, in the Keraḷa region, where he was raising his son Śivaguru according to the ancient traditions.

Śivaguru, who was to become Śaṅkara's father, was sent at an early age was sent to a Vedic school (*pāṭhaśālā*). At the end of his studies, he asked his parents for permission to continue studying the Veda and to lead an ascetic life (*brahmacārin*). However they persuaded him to renounce this and chose a spouse in the village of Pāḷur, of the same social order into which he had been born. Śivaguru, according to the ancient Vedic rites, was thus wed to Āryāmbā...

Even though the couple were leading a rigorously orthodox life, and despite the frequent fasting that Śivaguru and Āryāmbā were enduring, it did not seem as if the gods wanted to further favor their home. One has to remember that in traditional India the birth of a descendant, and particularly a son, was regarded as essential, as after the death of the parents, he could perform the annual funerary rites and the sacrificial offerings to the *Mani*.

While they were in Trichūr, where the went on a pilgrimage with the purpose of imploring for the grace of an heir, Lord Śiva, satisfied with their austerities (*tapas*), appeared to them in a dream and left to them the choice of his blessings: either many children of average intelligence, but all endowed with long life, or a single child of short life but who would be the glory not only of their family, and their community, but of India and of the world.

In the morning, after Śivaguru and Āryāmbā, had described their respective dreams to each other, they went to the temple of Vaṭakkunnātha and asked the God to shed light. Śiva let them know that he himself was going to incarnate in this son, and that they had nothing else to do but go back to their village. Śivaguru and Āryāmbā then went back to Kālaṭi where they offered feasts to all the villagers and gave numerous gifts to all the poor people who lived nearby.

After some time, as Śiva himself had promised, light sprang from the person of Āryāmbā foretelling a happy event. As it is reported in the *Śaṅkaravijaya* ("Śaṅkara' triumphal journey"), at the child was born at midday on the fifth day of the clear fortnight in the month of *vaiśākha* (April-May), under the constellation of Punarvasu. The knowledgeable Nambūṭiri astrologers immediately checked his birth data and declared that all the planets were in favorable positions. On the eleventh day the name of Śaṅkara (Benefactor) was given to the child.

His biographers tell the story that, even before having been invested with the sacred thread (*upanayana*) at the age of five, Śaṅkara had already learned not only his maternal language, but also Sanskrit and had read both the greatest poems and the various cosmological and mythological accounts (*Purāṇa*). It is during this period that his father left this world. The little Śaṅkara tenderly consoled his mother who, after some time, sent him to complete his studies in the nearby *pāṭhaśālā* where he studied the Vedic *Saṁhitā* with the annexed six *Vedānga*: phonetics (*śikṣā*), rituals (*kalpa*), grammar (*vyākaraṇa*), etymology and lexicon (*nirukta*), prosody (*chandas*), and astronomy and astrology (*jyotiṣa*).

Visit of the Ascetics and the renouncing the world

After three years of study in the *pāṭhaśālā*, Śaṅkara had acquired, apart from the practice of the four Veda, a sound knowledge of the various Indian branches of traditional knowledge (*darśana*): Logic (*Tarka*), the *Yoga* of Patañjali, *Sāṁkhya* and *Pūrva Mımāṁsā*. At the age of eight he went back to live with his mother.

A short while later, some wandering ascetics (*saṁnyāsin*), as they were going through Kālaṭi, visited his home where they were very happy at the way they were received. One of them explained to Āryāmbā that, given the circumstances surrounding her son's birth, he was of age to leave this world but, thanks to the hospitality they had received, he was allowed to live a further eight years. The group, in which included both Agastaya and Nārada, blessed the home and left.

Āryāmbā suddenly remembered the words of God Śiva in Trichūr: «Either many children of average intelligence or this young Śaṅkara who will illumine the world». The ascetics had just finished saying that her only and beloved son would have died in eight years which meant at the age of sixteen. The young boy consoled his mother explaining that the relationship between parents and children in this life is transitory; the mutual emotional bonds are not supposed to be the main aim of our passage on this earth which is the Realization of the being and its Liberation...

After the Sages' visit Śaṅkara's inclination towards asceticism deepened every day. Āryāmbā therefore decided to divert his attention by getting him involved in house work, leading him to understand that she was going to look for a spouse for him. But in his daily meditations Śaṅkara intuited perfectly that he was destined to perform a great task, the greatest a son of India ever had to accomplish: to reestablish the teaching of the Veda in its original purity. How then could he persuade his mother, widow and furthermore without means, to let him leave?

One morning Śaṅkara went to the river to take his first swim of the day, when a crocodile grabbed him by a foot and dragged him into the current. Śaṅkara called his mother for help. Āryāmbā, trembling and scared, ran down on the bank of the Churna and saw her son struggling in the water. He called out/ made her understand that a crocodile had grabbed him by the leg. «O mother, if you grant me the permission to renounce the world, this crocodile will release me». Āryāmbā, rather than seeing her son die before her eyes, consented. Immediately the crocodile let go of him and Śaṅkara got to the shore. Filled with joy, he declared that from now on all women to whom he would ask for alms would be for him as many loving mothers, and the Master who would initiate him as a *saṁnyāsin* would be as a father for him, and his future disciples would be as his loving children. The entire sacred land of India and the entire world, and no longer just his small house of Kālaṭi, would become his abode...

Without turning back, the youth set off for Trichūr, through the rice fields and the plantations of coconut and arèca. Wrapped in his immaculate *mundu*, with the forehead, chest, and forearms marked with white ashes (*bhasma*), with the *rudrākṣa* necklace and the staff of a wandering monk, he could have been taken for Dakṣiṇāmūrti (Śiva) himself who, upon leaving the temple, started walking in the ways of India.

The encounter with Govinda

The majority of the biographies agree on the fact that this encounter took place near the source of the Narmadā river, which splashes full of whirlpools through wild scenery, its banks adorned by Śaiva sanctuaries, and the flows beside the low hills of Vindhya, which divide the Deccan from the Ganges plains. The site is known as Amarakaṇṭa or Amarakaṇṭaka, from the name of the nearby peak, which is also the name of the nearby village still today a pilgrimage destination... The ascetic Govinda used to sojourn in this sacred spot at regular intervals alternating his time there with periods spent in the Badarīnātha retreat in the Himālayas, at the feet of his Master, Gauḍapāda.

While Govinda was in Badarīnātha, he was ordered by Viṣṇu, in a dream, to move forward his departure and to go immediately to Amarakaṇṭa, where a new pupil of divine gifts was going to present himself. Waking up, he received the same instruction from Gauḍapāda, his master, and he hastened to obey...

Seeing a cave at the foot of a *vaṭa* tree, Śaṅkara wanders in and finds himself in front of an assembly of ascetics gathered around a venerable old man, profoundly absorbed in that state of concentration in which consciousness of any distinction between subject and object is absent and which is called "*samādhi*". Full of admiration, Śaṅkara goes clockwise three times around the cave, with hands joined in sign of respect, then, approaching Govinda, he prostrates himself in front of him and begins chanting a highly famous verse of salutation: «I bow to Govinda, supreme beatitude, my teacher» and continues with praises as to Ādiśeṣa, descended on earth first as Patañjali, and then in the present form. Coming out of *samādhi*, Govinda interrogates the child about his identity. Śaṅkara answers by composing on the spot the *Cidānanandastavarāja* or *Daśaslokī* (Hymn of praise of ten verses), where in elegant verse he negates identification with the material elements or with the mind, cognitive knowledge, the castes, the stages of life etc., reasserting in each stanza his identity with Śiva alone. The eyes of Govinda fill with tears of joy, and also Śaṅkara weeps. They tell each other the dreams that brought them to that encounter, and at the end the divine child asks Govinda to be his teacher... Quickly completing the customary preliminaries, Govinda initiates Śaṅkara communicating to him the four upaniṣadic aphorisms: «*Brahman* is Knowledge», «This *ātman* is *Brahman*», «That thou art» and «I am *Brahman*»...

The Masters lineage in which Śaṅkara entered, descending from Govinda, Gauḍapāda, Śuka and

Bādarāyaṇa, through the latter's Master Parāśara — a figure of some importance in the *Purāṇa* — was going back to the Vedic seer Vasiṣṭha, father of Parāśara (or of his father Śakti, depending on the version). The *Kevalādvaita* teaching came to Vasiṣṭha directly from Śiva or from Viṣṇu through Brahmā, depending on the Śaiva or Viṣṇuite traditional intonation.

The discipleship at the feet of Govinda

Śaṅkara's sojourn on the banks of the Narmadā was particularly fertile. The quick deepening of his knowledge of the *Kevalādvaita* doctrine, in which he soon surpassed both Govinda and his son Bhartṛprapañca, would leave its mark on a whole series of writings among which are the *Vivekacūḍāmaṇi* (The Great Jewel of Discernment) and the *Vākyavṛtti* (Expounding of the aphorism)...

The *Saṅkṣeapaśaṅkaravijaya* ("Concise exposition of Śaṅkara's triumphal course) introduces, at the end of the stay with Govinda, an episode destined to explain the departure to Varanasi and the drawing up of the *Brahmasūtrabhāṣya*: after a week of torrential rain, the Narmadā reach a level higher than its banks and flooded the a wide track of land, sweeping away villages and leaving many without a roof and desperate, while the storm raged on. Govinda was, as usual, immersed in meditation in the cave, when the waves of the flooding river, sweeping away all obstacles, rushed towards him. Śaṅkara then placed his alms bowl in front of the waters and pronounced the formula for "the attraction of the waters". The bowl swallowed up the advancing current until the river retreated back to its normal level. This amazing feet earned the youth not only the gratitude of the population who had been flooded, but made a deep impression on Govinda. In the past, during the rite of the sacred beverage, the *Soma*, which lasts one hundred days and was performed by the seer Atri on a peak of the Himālayas, Bādarāyaṇa had foretold to him that Śiva himself, descended in the world as his disciple, would write a worthy commentary to the *Brahmasūtra*. He would recognize him exactly because of the sudden stopping of the fury of the Narmadā which was threatening to swallow Amarkaṇṭa. Moved his Master instructed Śaṅkara to go to Varanasi and write there a commentary that would render clearly the message of those difficult aphorisms...

The *Bṛhacchaṅkaravijaya* (Śaṅkara Great Triumphal Journey) tells of Govinda putting in Śaṅkara's hands the verses Gauḍapāda wrote as commentary and appendix to the *Māṇḍūkya Upaniṣad*, known as *Āgamaśāstra*. The young man's enthusiasm was such that he begged Govinda to obtain from that sage the authorization to comment upon them. Master and disciple then were on their way to Badarīnātha, where Gauḍapāda, who by that time had attained the venerable age of one hundred and twenty, was carrying on with his teaching.

The sojourn in the Himalayas and the vision of Śiva

Badarīnātha is one of the most sacred pilgrimage sites of India, as it is located near the source of the Ganges (*Gaṅgodbheda*), the most pure of the rivers that sanctify the earth through their contact. Here the seers Nara and Nārāyaṇa, from whom two glittering twin peaks draw their names, had their hermitage, the Badarikāśrama...

As soon as they arrived, Govinda introduced the youth to the presence of Gauḍapāda. Śaṅkara prostrated himself at the feet of his teacher's teacher (*Paramaguru*), who welcomed him with gentleness and promised to teach him all he knew...

Having obtained the desired authorization to comment upon the *Āgamaśāstra*, Śaṅkara did it with such satisfaction on the part of Gauḍapāda that he instructed him to comment the threefold Canon of *Vedānta* in full. For the following four years the young man dedicated himself to this work, concluding his effort with the *Brahmasūtrabhāṣya*. He was by now sixteen, and his works had all been accomplished; the following sixteen years of his life were going to be devoted to the spreading of the teaching. But before starting on the second half of his earthly wandering, Śaṅkara was going to be submitted to an investiture more solemn than the ones he had already received in his native village on the banks of the Narmadā. Gauḍapāda in fact decided to introduce the young man to his own Guru, Śuka, and to his *Paramaguru*, Bādarāyaṇa himself, who at the time were meditating on the top of mount Kailāsa...

On the occasion of the meeting with the two venerable old men, Śaṅkara expressed his joy by composing the *Dhanyāṣṭaka* or *Dhanyastotra* (Eight verses on the Blessed), a hymn in their praise. His exposition of the *Brahmasūtrabhāṣya* filled them with enthusiasm, and they declared that he had perfectly grasped and expressed the transcendent Reality of the *Upaniṣad*...

Bādarāyaṇa and Śuka urged Śaṅkara to go to Varanasi, the center of the Indian culture of the classical period, and to spread the doctrine from there and refute the heterodox schools. The three teachers then blessed their worthy successor and disappeared: with his advent their earthly mission had come to a close.

Śaṅkara remained alone. The three wise men had dissolved as in a dream, and the totality of human existence revealed itself in its true nature at that moment: insubstantial, and absurd, similar to a cheap illusionist show. His pain at the departure of his spiritual guides left room for a total detachment and for an ardent aspiration to do away with all illusion. These inner dispositions are the premise for the liberating experience of the divine Master. Thanks to them, Śaṅkara became perfectly attuned with his own transcendent archetype, and the deep solitude of that peak battered by the wind blossomed into a marvelous vision. Śaṅkara saw in front of him a youth of superhuman beauty, seated at the foot of a vaṭa tree under the shadow of a tabernacle covered with fragrant flowers. He had three eyes and the crescent moon in his braided hair formed a tiara, and his body was white as milk, resplendent with inner light like a crystal. A snake of deep sapphire blue was coiling around his neck, in between the string of pearls that were hanging down his chest. In three of his four hands he was holding a rosary of pure pearls, a bowl filled with red *amṛta*, the beverage of immortality, and a closed book. The fourth hand was resting on his heart, symbolic gesture of eternal knowledge. Around were rows of white-haired seers who were sitting full of respect, in contemplation of the God.

Śiva was manifesting himself to his own *Avatāra* in the form of Dakṣiṇāmūrti, the hypostasis of total knowledge and eloquent silence. Śaṅkara went into *samādhi* contemplating the totally serene appearance of the vision; when he came out of that ineffable state beyond any duality, he prostrated before the supreme Master chanting the *Dakṣiṇāmūrtistotra* (Hymn to Dakṣiṇāmūrti), which he composed there and then. Among the venerable sages encircling Śiva, Śuka came forward and interceded for the disciple of the disciple of his own disciple: Śaṅkara was worthy to receive the highest initiation. Śiva consented in a silent smile. His assistants immediately carried out the necessary preparations. Śaṅkara was sprinkled by them with water from the Ganges and subjected to the customary purifications. With his body smeared with ashes, he wore a new robe of the wandering ascetic and, holding in one hand the staff and in the other the alms bowl, he solemnly renounced all desire, committing to perfect obedience to the will of the immortal Master. He then proceeded to the feet of Śiva and adored Him composing there and then the five verses of the *Parāpūjā*.

The divine Master then communicated to him the teaching on the absolute, the essence of the *Upaniṣad*, in the same pregnant formulas that Govinda used in the initiation transmission six years earlier. Śaṅkara repeated them devoutly, absorbed in their meaning. During the ceremony, the youth took the *Adhyātmasaṃnyāsa* – the renouncer's condition that identifies with the supreme consciousness, detached from all its contents – becoming a *Paramahaṃsaparivrājaka*, wandering monk of the highest level within the brāhmaṇic orthodoxy. At the end of the ceremony he received from the shining form of Śiva the book he was holding in his hand. He opened it, and looking through the pages, he realized it contained the exact text of his *Brahmasūtrabhāṣya*. One cannot imagine a more explicit confirmation of the level of the work: in the symbolism of the figure of Dakṣiṇāmūrti, the book is the synthesis of the liberating knowledge, tangible form of the divine omniscience!... Śaṅkara returned to Badarīnātha transfigured: now he was really the Master of the world (*Jagadguru*), given his mission in a full and perfect way.

Śaṅkara restores the Vedic Tradition

At the beginning of the eighth century *Pūrva Mīmāṁsā* was the most influential orthodox school, principally interpreting the Veda mainly from a ritualistic point of view (*karma kāṇḍa*) and as the code for the duties of the individual (*dharma*).

In that period Kumārila Bhaṭṭa, one of the greatest *Mīmāṁsaka* Masters who ever existed was living in Prayāga (today's Allahabad) approximately 80 miles west of Varanasi. According to the tradition, Kumārila was an incarnation of Subrhmaṇya, second son of Śiva and Pārvatī, who had incarnated into him to re-establish the Vedic Tradition vis à vis the Buddhism that was in decline at the time. When still very young, although born of a brāhmaṇic family, Kumārila succeeded in being accepted into a Buddhist monastery (*vihāra*) where he studied all the heterodox doctrines. As soon as he left the *vihāra* Kumārila, having learned in depth the subjects and the points of doctrine of the Buddhists, refuted them publicly, solemnly re-establishing the validity of the Vedic rite.

Śaṅkara sincerely admired the courageous work performed by Kumārila, but could not share his *Mīmāṁsaka* positions regarding God's existence. In his enormous task of re-establishing the authority of the Veda, Kumārila Bhaṭṭa had several times maintained that it was not necessary to postulate an omniscient and omnipresent God. The Master of Kālaṭi thus went to Prayāga to meet Kumārila, to persuade him of the truth of the Advaita vision and, if possible, have him adhere to this vision.

Upon arriving in Prayāga, where the three sacred rivers meet (Gaṅgā, Yamunā and Sarasvatī), Śaṅkara learned that Kumārila had just begun an atonement rite (*Agnikuṇḍa*). In fact he, in his intense effort to re-establish the Vedic doctrine, he had committed two very serious errors. Firstly, when still young, he had passed himself off as a Buddhist and had made it into a monastery as such: thus he had lied to the guru and publicly betrayed the teaching he had received. And secondly, tenaciously defending the *Mīmāṁsaka* point of view, he had denied God's existence many times.

Kumārila had decided to remedy his two errors by sacrificing himself on a pyre to which he himself had set fire. His physical body was starting to burn when Śaṅkara arrived in Triveṇī. The great *Mīmāṁsaka* Master, while remaining totally conscious at the center of the flames, told him that, once the process of expiation had started he could not turn back. Up to the end Kumārila kept total control of his faculties and readiness of spirit, declaring that he was glad to spend his last moments together with a follower of Tradition (*smārta*) and to approve the non-dualist theses. Finally he suggested that Śaṅkara should meet another great *Mīmāṁsaka*, Maṇḍana Miśra, with whom he would be able to debate his view points.

Śaṅkara went therefore to Māhiṣmatī (northern Bihār) and because Maṇḍana Miśra was performing the ceremony of the *śṛaddha* for the *Mani* found the doors to the house were closed; but Śaṅkara utilizing his yogic powers (*siddhi*), entered the place.

When Maṇḍana Miśra, who was against the practice of renouncing the world, saw Śaṅkara appearing in front of him in his ochre robe he asked him on whose authority a *saṁnyāsin*, who had nothing any longer to do with the domestic rites, came to upset the progress of the ceremony being offered to the *Mani*. A bitter contest developed. The *Brāhmana* officiating with Maṇḍana Miśra, though in agreement with him, nevertheless brought to his attention that a *saṁnyāsin* who is there to beg is a person worthy of taking part in Viṣṇu's ceremony of *śraddha*. They asked Maṇḍana Miśra to forget the incident and to invite the saṁnyāsin to participate in their meal. Śaṅkara's answer was the he had not come to beg for food (*anna bhikṣa*), but to beg for knowledge (*vāda bhikṣa*) in a philosophical debate with Maṇḍana Miśra.

Having established the obligations of the defeated, whoever that might be, the two participants began their debate on the dawn of the following day. The condition was that in case Maṇḍana Miśra was the loser he would immediately embrace the *Advaita Vedānta*, and that, should Śaṅkara be defeated, he would have to renounce his non-dual positions, wear the white clothes of the *Mīmāṁsaka* and from then on accept the points of view of the ritualists. The umpire of the debate was Sarasvatī, Maṇḍana Miśra's wife, who was appreciated for her fineness of knowledge. Sarasvatī put around the neck of both a wreath of fresh flowers and on leaving the room of the debate announced that he whose wreath withered first would be declared the loser. At the end of the sixth day Maṇḍana Miśra, due to the irrefutable expositions given by Śaṅkara, was short on arguments and started losing ground in the debate. Shortly thereafter, the wreath he was wearing around his neck started to wither. In the end Maṇḍana Miśra had to concede victory, and as established on the first day of the debate, asked to be initiated and became *saṁnyāsin*. Śaṅkara gave him the name of Sureśvara. Sarasvatī, as the faithful Hindu wife she was, renounced the world and entered a female community.

By visiting all the sacred (*tīrtha*) sites and making the most important pilgrimages (*yātrā*), Śaṅkara ceaselessly promoted debates with the representatives of both heterodox and orthodox schools. His purpose was not to make of the supporters of the other schools into converts to the *Advaita*, as if proselytizing, but rather to establish unity and peace in India. The Non-duality Doctrine, the *Kevalādavaita*, is founded on the authority of the *Śruti*. Śaṅkara interprets the *Upaniṣad* by using pure reason; his implacable logic demolishes all argumentation. The *Advaita Vedānta* is not a doctrine that comes to vie with the other schools be they orthodox or heterodox. On the contrary, without opposing them, *Advaita Vedānta* illumines them from within and shows everybody that a sole Truth polarizes the entire whole. Indeed the points of view of both the *Sāṁkhya* and of the *Mīmāṁsaka* as well as the Buddhist and *Jaina* points of view are valid provided they do not lose sight of the supreme Reality (*Brahmādvaita*).

Śaṅkara did not limit himself to fighting those heresies that infiltrated traditional Hinduism. Faced with the decadence of rites and customs – in some sanctuaries, apart from bloody sacrifices, under the pretext of unifying the masculine and the feminine aspects of the divine, actual orgies were taking place – he established radical religious reforms.

For this purpose, he instituted ten ascetic Orders (*daśanāmī*), so as to witness throughout the whole of India, by exemplary living, to the continuity of the *Advaita* Tradition.

Subsequently he established monasteries (*maṭha*) where the teaching of the *Śruti* (heard Tradition) and of the *Smṛti* (recalled Tradition) could be given through a succession of spiritual Masters (*jagadguru*) surrounded by Advaitin Masters (*ācārya*) and by several Sages and learned ones (*paṇḍit*) who would constantly keep the Tradition alive. He positioned these monasteries at the four corners of the sub-continent: in the Kāthiyāvār peninsula, at Dvārakā, the town where god Kṛṣṇa once reigned; at Badarīnātha, in the Himālayas; at Jagannāthapurī in Orissa; on the banks of the Tuṇgabhadrā, at Śṛiṅgeri in Maïsūr and in Kāñcīpuram in Tamilnāḍu. In his native land of Keraḷa, his disciples established three *maṭha* in Trichūr, one of the holy places in India where today the *Ṛgveda Saṁhitā* are taught.

From Rāmeśvaram to the Himālayas Śaṅkara visited the great Hindu temples of all persuasions. What was important for him was not so much the way, or the personal deity (*iṣṭa devatā*), but the intensity of the faith, and the sincerity with which, through a deity, the supreme Knowledge was aspired to. The level of rituals, which are but acts and prayers producing just a momentary pacification of the mind, must sooner or later be gone beyond in order to attain the vision of the sole Being.

The mahāsamādhi

On the morning of the eleventh day of the clear half of the lunar month of *vaiśākha* (April-May) in the year *raktākṣin* (58th of the Indian cycle of 60), according to the *Bṛhacchaṅkaravijaya*, Śaṅkara announced to his disciples that he had decided to abandon his body. If they still had some doubts, they could present them to him before his death. They gathered around him, and each one of them recounting to himself all the points of Doctrine that still remained obscure. Before speaking they gazed for the last time upon Śaṅkara's smiling face, and lo, his simple look was enough to dispel all the knots in their hearts: not even one of them was left with a pending argument requiring further explanation. Then, in the pervading silence, Sudhanvabhūti asked Śaṅkara to summarize the essence of his teachings. The Master consented. He recounted that once, at the request of Govinda, he had composed six stanzas on a theme requested by this regal disciple, and he would now recite them in their presence. He then began to chant the solemn *Nirvāṇaṣaṭka*.

Once the hymn was over, he declared that he would be present every time they remembered him and in every place where the *Kevalādvaita* was going to be taught or meditated upon. Then, as he was sitting there, he entered meditation...

The *Saṅkṣepaśaṅkaravijaya* states that from Kāśmīr Śaṅkara went to Kedāranātha by way of Badarīnātha, and from there flew to the Kailāsa, resuming his true Śiva appearance. Among the praises of the gods led by Indra and Viṣṇu, under a rain of celestial flowers, Brahmā offered his arm and he ascended on his divine bull, Nandin, on whose back he proceeded towards his transcendent throne, among the joyful cries of the Seers and with all the cool splendor of the moon in his braided hair. The *Śaṅkaravijayavilāsa* narrates how in Badarīnātha Dattātreya appeared, and taking Śaṅkara by the hand, led him in his cave nearby, from where he was never seen emerging.

Anantānandagiri in his Śaṅkaravijaya states: «Under the form of all pervading Consciousness He still lives today. In truth, He is the Guru Śaṅkarācārya, who grants Liberation to those who are ready».

We conclude this short writing on the life of Śaṅkara with some words from Martin-Dubost's book: «The paradox of Śaṅkara: his life seems to contradict his teaching. The Master who preached renouncing the world and non-action, did not retire in his cave on the Himālayas, but traveled ceaselessly throughout the entire country, wrote continuously, instructed his disciples and divulged the *Advaita* doctrine.

Direct descendant of Yājñavalkya, the great upaniṣadic Sage, Śaṅkara is the symbol of the "triumphant action". He reflected Kṛṣna's statements in the *Bhagavadgītā* (III, 22):

"O Pārtha, there is nothing in the three worlds that has to be done by Me nor anything I should have or that has not been resolved; nevertheless I find myself acting [though remaining detached]"».

The passages of Śaṅkara's life are from the following books: Paul Martin-Dubost, "Śaṅkara and the Vedānta" (*His Life, Visit of the Ascetics and the renouncing the world, Śaṅkara restores the Vedic Tradition*) and, Mario Piantelli, "Śaṅkara and the Kevalādvaita" (*Before being born, The encounter with Govinda, The discipleship at the feet of Govinda, The stay in the Himālayas and the vision of Śiva, The mahāsamādhi*). Both books are Italian Editions, and published by Edizioni Āśram Vidyā, Rome.

GAUḌAPĀDA AND ŚAṄKARA IN THE ADVAITA TRADITION

With Gauḍapāda begins what has been called the *mānavasampradāya*, the transmission of the teaching through human beings.

It is with Gauḍapāda that the *Advaita* Tradition becomes historically evident as the visible manifestation of an already existing Tradition. He was the first human teacher to receive the *Advaita* knowledge and to teach it to his disciples; for this fact he is paid the highest respect within the *Advaita* Tradition.

Śaṅkara acknowledges that the spiritual and philosophical heritage of the *Advaita Vedānta*, which was already present in the Upaniṣad, comes from the teaching transmitted through a succession of gurus (*guru-paramparā*).

They are recalled in a Hymn, the *Paramparāstotra*, which includes the list of the early A*dvaita* teachers and that is recited by the Śaṅkarian followers when they begin the study of the Great Commentaries. Here it is:

> *«Nārayāṇaṁ padmabhuvaṁ vāsiṣṭhaṁ śaktiṁ ca tatputraṁ parāśaraṁ ca | vyāsaṁ śukaṁ gauḍapādaṁ mahāntaṁ govindaṁ yogīndram athāsya śiṣyaṁ | śrıśaṅkarācāryamathāsya padmapādaṁ ca hastāmalakaṁ ca śiṣyam | taṁ toṭakaṁ vārtikakāramanyanasmadgurūnsantata mānato 'smi».*

> «To Nārāyaṇa, to the lotus-born [Brahmā], to Vāsiṣṭha, to Śakti and to his son Parāśara, to Vyāsa, to Śuka, to great Gauḍapāda, to Govinda-Yogīndra and to his disciple Śrı Śaṅkarācārya, then to his disciples Padmapāda, Hastāmalaka, Toṭaka, Vārtikakāra [Sureśvara], to these our Masters we pay our respectful homage now and forever».

The lineage of succession from Nārāyaṇa to Śuka is called *vaṁśarṣiparamparā* or from father to son, and the one from Śuka onwards *śiṣyaparamparā*, from teacher to disciple.

The greatness of Gauḍapāda's is testified by Śaṅkara who at the end of his commentary to the *Māṇḍūkyakārikā* addresses the following salutation to the Author of the *Kārikā* calling him *paramaguru*, an expression that is to be interpreted as the recognition of the spiritual lineage and the authority of "supreme Master" due to his profound knowledge of the *Veda*:

> «I prostrate before the Master of my Master (*paramaguru*), the most venerable among the venerables who, seeing the beings immersed in the ocean of this world – an ocean infested by frightening sharks

such as birth and death – out of compassion towards all beings, has given this nectar, which is difficult to drink even for the Gods, and that lies in the depths of the great sea. This is the *Veda*, *Veda* that he unveils by the power of his enlightened intellect».

Gauḍapāda's authority is recognized also by other commentators: Sureśvara, a direct disciple of Śaṅkara, in the *Naiśkarmyasiddhi* (Realization through the renouncing of action) mentions two *Kārikā* and in the *Bṛhadāraṇyakopaniṣadbhāṣyavārttika* explicitly cites Gauḍapāda several times. Vidyāraṇya in the *Pañcadaśī* (the Fifteen Chapters) and in the *Jīvanmuktiviveka* (Liberation in Life) makes direct reference to the *Ācārya* Gauḍapāda and his teachings. Finally Sadānanda in the *Vedāntasāra* (The Essence of *Vedānta*) uses verses taken from both the *Māṇḍūkya Upaniṣad* and the *Kārikā*.

ŚAṄKARA'S WORKS

Śaṅkara's writings can be classified in three main groups: "Commentaries" (*bhāṣya*, *vivaraṇa*, *ṭīkā*), "Hymns" (*stotra* and *stuti*) , and "Specific Treaties" (*prakaraṇagrantha*). Some of Śaṅkara's works have been published by Edizioni Āśram Vidyā, and due to their fundamental importance among them are the Commentaries to the *Brahmasūtra* of Bādarāyaṇa and to the *Māṇḍūkyakārikā* of Gauḍapāda.

Śaṅkara's Commentary upon the Brahmasūtra

The Brahmasūtra comprises a collection of 555 Aphorisms (*sūtra*) in which the compiler, Bādarāyaṇa (at times identified with Vyāsa, the *Ṛṣi* who put into order the texts of the *Veda*, the *Mahābhārata* and the *Purāṇa*) codified the *Vedānta* teaching expounded in the *Upaniṣad*.

The text of the *Brahmasūtra* is divided into four Chapters (*adhyāya*): "Concordance" (*samanvaya*), "Absence of Contradiction" (*avirodha*), "Spiritual Discipline" (*sādhana*), and "The Fruit" (*phala*). Every chapter is made up of four Parts (*pāda*) and each one of these is structured in various Propositions (*adhikaraṇa*).

Given the extremely concise and synthetic form, the *Brahmasūtra* presents difficulties in interpretation if it is read without a commentary. By clarifying issues, modalities and references, a commentary provides a real aid to the understanding of the text.

Śaṅkara's Commentary is indispensable for the comprehension of the *Advaita Vedānta*, not only due to its direct emanation, which finds in Bādarāyana-Vyāsa the primary source of the *Sūtra* themselves, but also because of the doctrinal purpose expressed by Śaṅkara in his elucidation of the teaching.

Śaṅkara's commentary offers a complete treatment of the subjects addressed by the Sūtra and explores every argument or objection that could possibly be raised. He explains in a truly exhaustive and satisfactory way every possible question and at the same time dispels any possible doubt which might arise.

Professor Tucci in his *Storia della filosofia Indiana* writes as follows: «Śaṅkara's task was remarkably different from that of the commentators of other systems... First of all these *Sūtra* could lend themselves to different and discordant interpretations. This is, in fact, proven by the variety of tendencies they inspired and that were stemming equally from the same source, each one arrogating to itself the claim to be the faithful interpreter... And it was indeed necessary to reconcile the *Sūtra* with the Upaniṣadic literature, which was neither organic or homogeneous, not only because there was no trace of a system, but above all because, being born in different schools and compiled at different times, it had always undergone the influence of new currents of thought... Therefore, Śaṅkara's task could not be limited to that of a simple commentator; he had to defend the authority of the *Upaniṣad* and provide homogeneity to what if nothing else, appeared to be discrepancies, find in them the same ideas that the Sūtra had codified and justify with their revelation the foundations of his own system».

The Māṇḍūkyakārikā of Gauḍapāda with Śaṅkara's Commentary

Gauḍapāda, having risen to the highest peaks of realization, saw that the ultimate Reality can neither be born nor can it die, and with the support of the Nārāyaṇa-Principle was able to unveil for the first time to humanity beings in a clear and concise way the *Ajātivāda*, the doctrine of "non-generation", and the *Asparśayoga*, the yoga of "no-support or relation". These Teachings were already present in the *Śruti* but were not recognized by yogis and seekers because none of them had risen with their consciousness to the apex of the *Advaita* realization.

In order to expound the *Ajātivāda* and the *Asparśayoga* Gauḍapāda chose to comment upon the *Māṇḍūkya Upaniṣad*. The *Upaniṣad* deals with the three states of Being (*Virāṭ*, *Hiraṇyagarbha*, *Īśvara*) and the Fourth state or *Turīya* which is the absolute Reality. The doctrine and philosophy of the *Māṇḍūkya* is the most meaningful and profound *Upaniṣad* of *Advaita Vedānta* and, on its own, constitutes the very foundation of metaphysical realization. The *Mukti Upaniṣad* in this respect states: «If the goal is the attainment of the supreme truth, then the *Māṇḍūkya Upaniṣad* alone is altogether sufficient».

Gauḍapāda divided his commentary (*kārikā*) into four chapters called respectively: *Āgama prakaraṇ a* (chapter based on the Holy Scriptures), *Vaitathya prakaraṇa* (the absolute non-reality of empirical experience), *Advaita prakaraṇa* (non-duality) and *Alātaśānti prakaraṇa* (the extinction of the burning ember).

He states that there is an unchangeable Reality, eternal, in act, devoid of generation and extinction, without cause-effect, outside of time-space and non-contradictory, which is One-without-a-second. Since Reality is a constant and perfect unity, all differentiation, multiplicity, impermanence and change cannot be the ultimate and supreme Reality but only appearance or, representation, which acquires reality only when viewed from the standpoint of "opinion".

Gauḍapāda sets out from the standpoint of the Absolute or the One-without-a-second and comes to the following conclusion: «The supreme truth is this: there is no birth and no dissolution, no aspirant to liberation and no liberated, and no one who is in bondage»[1]

Śaṅkara takes up the *Advaita-Asparśa* theme of Gauḍapāda. In his turn he expounds it with great dialectical accuracy never to be equalled nor exceeded, and in his *Vivekacūḍāmaṇi* comes to the same conclusion[1].

It is appropriate to point out that these daring statements are not to be mistaken for either the subjective idealism or the nihilism of certain philosophical currents.

Due to their importance the *kārikā* of Gauḍapāda have been commented upon by the great Śaṅkara, and this how Raphael underlines the importance of this event: «This is of a particular significance because the two greatest representatives of *Advaita* met on the plane of the doctrine, and not only of the doctrine, making a truly decisive contribution to the metaphysics of *Vedānta*».

---

[1] See, Śaṅkara, *Vivekacūḍāmaṇi*, The Crest Jewel of Discernment, Translation from the Sanskrit and Commentary by Raphael, *sūtra* 574. Aurea Vidyā. New York.

HIS TEACHING

In order to "comprehend" Śaṅkara's message in its real significance it is necessary to bear in mind some fundamental notes:

a) Śaṅkara did not come to destroy but rather to build and the philosophy he taught must not be considered as opposing the other schools of thought. Gauḍapāda, Śaṅkara's *paramaguru* (spiritual Master), had already maintained in his *Māṇḍūkyakārikā* that there could not be any antagonism between the *Advaita* (Non-duality) and the dualistic philosophies. In the same way as you cannot go into a fight against your own limbs, similarly the *Advaita* cannot have any opposition with the various philosophical points of view.

b) In a time of confusion and of crisis, Śaṅkara dedicated his short but intense life to the noble end of "revivifying" the Vedic-Upaniṣadic Tradition and pointing to that path to Liberation (*mokṣa*) which is based on Knowledge as already indicated by the *Upaniṣad*.

Śaṅkara defines himself as an *aupaniṣada*, i.e. follower of the *Upaniṣad*, in that they teach self-knowledge and liberation from ignorance (*avidyā*). In the *Upadeśasāhasrī* Śaṅkara states:

> «This Instruction, which summarizes the essence of the *Upaniṣad*, has been composed in order to impart the knowledge of *Brahman*, so that ignorance may be totally destroyed and transmigratory existence may be definitively extinguished».
>
> «The word *Upaniṣad* derives from the root *sad* [to sit], and to this undetermined form the particles *upa* [near] and *ni* [down] are added. In this way, all that liberates from class bondage, etc. and that destroys birth [death], etc. takes the name of *upaniṣad*»[1] .

Śaṅkara is considered from many perspectives as a philosopher, a mystic, an exegete of the *Śruti*, a founder of monastic orders (maṭha), an *Avatāra* (incarnation of Śiva), a national hero, a master of one of the utmost realizations of the human spirit, an ocean of Wisdom and the glory of India. But above all, he is to be recognized as the supreme Instructor (*Ācārya*) who was able to indicate the true and supreme end of human existence (and not only human): the Liberation (*mokṣa*) from *saṁsāra*-becoming and the recognition of our own real nature.

---

[1] Śaṅkara, *Upadeśasāhasrī*, The Instruction in a Thousand Verses: II,I, 25-26. Translation from the Sanskrit and Commentary by the Kevala Group. Edizioni Āśram Vidyā. Rome. (Italian Edition).

Martin-Dubost writes: «He did not invent Non-dualism [already present in the *Upaniṣad*]... he made use of his Vedāntin predecessors, among which Gauḍapāda holds a place of honor. Nevertheless his genius stands out for the way in which He has been able to harmonize certain (apparently) contradictory passages of the *Upaniṣad* and constitute a coherent doctrine... Śaṅkara does not intend to limit himself to demonstrations, however brilliant, but aims at liberating the mind, relying for this purpose on the validity of his method. One of the reflections on the theme portrays well his care *(Upadeśasāhasrī*: II, XVIII, 3): "Were it impossible to realize the awareness 'I myself am pure Being, eternally free', to what avail would the *Śruti* infuse the teaching through listening, etc. with a care that is comparable only to that of a mother?"».

Śaṅkara, always faithful to the *Upaniṣad*, states that knowledge alone leads to Liberation; what is imprisoning is *avidyā*, i.e. ignorance concerning the real nature of Being, and therefore it is only through a knowledge of metaphysical order that ignorance can be defeated. This Knowledge implies a profound transformation, a realizative *sādhanā* the phases of which are nothing but moments of transformation-transfiguration of the entity, as a result of attainments of consciousness, or "recognitions", since the entity already has in himself the absolute Knowledge: That thou art (*Tat tvam asi*) states the *Chāndogya Upaniṣad*.

To follow this Way certain qualifications are required and Śaṅkara presents these in his *Vivekacūḍāmaṇi*:

viveka or discernment between the Real and the non-real, *vairāgya* or the detachment from the non-real recognizing it as such, the six virtues of the mind and *mumukṣutā* or the intense aspiration to Liberation.

We quote several of the *sūtra* from the *Vivekacūḍāmaṇi* in which Śaṅkara expounds these qualifications:

«*Viveka* is the discernment between real and unreal and is founded on the unshakable conviction that *Brahman* alone is real and that the phenomenal universe is non-real»

«*Vairāgya* is the detachment from all transitory enjoyments, from the corporeal ones to those corresponding to the state of Brahmā. Renouncing, based on personal reflection and on the teaching of the *guru* must be applied to all the organs and to all conditions of enjoyment»

«*Śama* is the condition of the pacified mind which constantly contemplates the aim [*Brahman*], after having detached from the multiplicity of sensory objects because it has revealed their emptiness»

«*Dama*, or self control, is there when one detaches the two groups of sensory organs from their corresponding objects, bringing them back to their respective centers. Recollection is considered perfect (*uparati*) when the external objects stop activating one's modifications of the mind (*vṛtti*)»

«*Titikṣā*, or patience, is that condition able to accept afflictions without resentment or rebellion, since it is free of any anxiety and any lamentation»

«*Śraddhā* is the trustful adherence [faith] to the truth expounded in the Scriptures and by one's own *guru*; through it one arrives at apprehending the real»

«*Samādhāna*, or mental strength, is that condition in which the *buddhi* is constantly concentrated on the absolute *Brahman*, without falling into mental plays»

«*Mumukṣutā*, or yearning for emancipation, is the determination to apprehend one's own real nature, liberating oneself from all those types of bondage which are created by ignorance, from those relating to the sense of ego to those relating to the gross body»[1]

---

[1] Śaṅkara, *Vivekacūḍāmaṇi*, The Crest Jewel of Discernment, Translation from the Sanskrit and Commentary by Raphael, *sūtra* 20-27. Op. cit.

PLATO AND ŚAṄKARA

Although the historical settings of Plato and of Śaṅkara are very different, it is possible to find, behind the diversity, significant parallels.

Both Plato and Śaṅkara lived during times of confusion and spiritual muddle. Both Philosophers had the role of confronting this confusion by indicating their unshakable trust in Knowledge, the way leading to the "Supreme Good".

We quote some passages from Raphael's work, *Initiation into the Philosophy of Plato* in which the concordances between the Doctrine of Plato and the *Advaita Vedānta* of Śaṅkara are highlighted:

«Śaṅkara and Plato stand as "rectifiers" of *Vedānta* and the *Mysteries* Visions respectively, which were both degraded by the hands of priests not qualified to fulfil their functions. Thus they both act within the scope of a precise renewal of the religious Tradition, reintegrating it in its original purity. Both extend the spiritual Vision beyond caste individualism, and indeed *Polis*, restoring vigor to the universal vision of Being. From this stems the development of the "Greater Mysteries" or of *Paravidyā* (supreme knowledge, as distinct from *aparavidyā* or relative, secondary knowledge).

The two Teachings postulate an absolute Constant as *causa sui*, on which the Whole depends.

They give the same definition of the term "reality". The Real is that which is permanent, unchangeable and *universally* valid, that which has neither origin nor end, that which is *identical* to itself.

Plato, like Śaṅkara, identifies Being, Identity and Immobility with the supreme Good; while becoming, variation and motion with the empirical sensible...

They conceive of conflict, of pain and of the contradictions of the human condition as the effect of a fall-oblivion-*avidyā*...

The two masters live, write and act in accordance with the Teaching they profess.

From the Greater Mysteries of Traditional order Plato primarily draws out the metaphysical content, which is for the few, while leaving to the many the more ritualistic and preparatory content (Lesser Mysteries)... Similarly Śaṅkara leaves aside the Vedic ritualism of the *Mımāṁsā* in order to give expression to the essentially metaphysical part (*paravidyā*) of the *Veda-Upaniṣad*.

In as much as it is traditional and sacred philosophy, it is of a cathartic, realizative order, which both Plato and Śaṅkara assert unequivocally. This shows that both Plato and Śaṅkara did not write for the sake of mere "discursiveness" as an end in itself, but to point out a "road", a "way" of realization, of salvation, of liberation of the Soul from the shackles of ignorance.

Both Teachings strike an optimistic note and offer great philosophical comfort; humans can raise themselves up from their spiritual, psychological, and material debasement and solve all their existential problems; they can thus escape the grip of suffering and contradiction in which they live»[1] .

---

[1] Raphael, *Initiation into the Philosophy of Plato.* Ch. Platonism and Vedānta. Aurea Vidyā. New York.

AUREA VIDYĀ COLLECTION

Books by Raphael

At the Source of Life

Beyond the illusion of the ego

Initiation into the Philosophy of Plato

Orphism and the Initiatory Tradition

Tat tvam asi, That thou art, The Path of Fire According to the Asparśavāda

The Threefold Pathway of Fire

Traditional Classics

Śaṅkara, *Ātmabodha**, Self-knowledge

Śaṅkara, *Drigdriśyaviveka**, Discernment between *ātman* and non-*ātman*

Gauḍapāda, *Māṇḍūkyakārikā**, The Māṇḍūkya Upaniṣad with the **verses**-*kārikā* of Gauḍapāda and Commentary by Raphael

Parmenides, *On the Order of Nature*, Περί φύσεως**, For a Philosophical Ascesis

Śaṅkara, *Vivekacūḍāmaṇi**, The Crest-jewel of Discernment

Other Books by Raphael
published in English

Essence and Purpose of Yoga
The Initiatory Pathways to the Transcendent
Element Books, Shaftesbury, U.K.

Pathway of Fire, Initiation to the Kabbalah
S. Weiser, York Beach, Maine, U.S.A.

The Pathway of Non-duality, Advaitavāda
Motilal Banarsidass, New Delhi.

Forthcoming Publications
by Aurea Vidyā

Patañjali, *The Regal Way to Realization**, Yogadarśana

Śaṅkara, *Aparokṣānubhūti**, Self-realization

Raphael, *The Science of Love*

*The Bhagavadgītā**

Bādarāyaṇa, *Brahmasūtra**

*Five Upaniṣads**, Īśa, Kaivalya, Sarvasāra, Amṛtabindu, Atharvaśira

Plotinus, *The Enneads: An Anthology.* Edited by G. Faggin.

* Translated from the Sanskrit, and Commented, by Raphael

** Edited by Raphael

BIOGRAPHIES OF THE MASTERS

Śaṅkara

Forthcoming Biographies

Ṛṣi

Parmenides

Gauḍapāda

Pythagoras

Plato

Plotinus

* * *

www.ingramcontent.com/pod-product-compliance
Lightning Source LLC
Chambersburg PA
CBHW031615040426
42452CB00006B/541
9781931406116